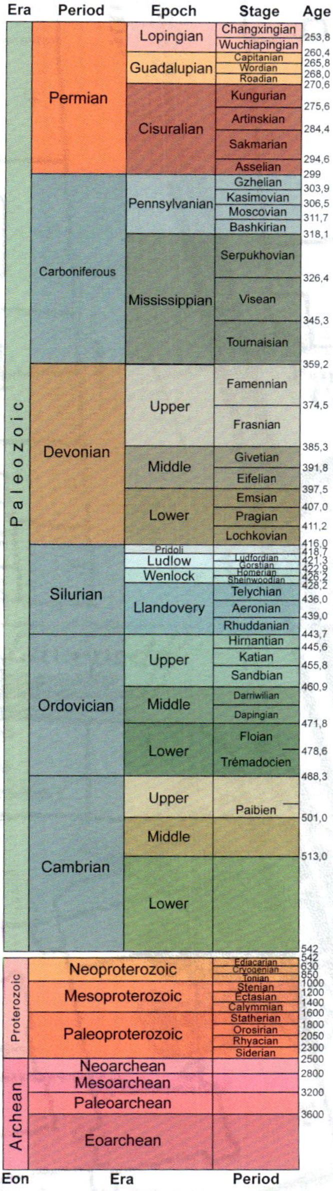

Rhyolite from Trente

Granite from Clarté

Granite from Flamanville
Slate from Mael Carhaix

Marble from Lunel
Belgian black marble

Granite from Plaintel
Limestone from Soignies

Griotte marble from Pyrénées

Red marble from Languedoc

Slate from Angers

Granite from Vire

INTRODUCTION

According to some experts, the original Lutetia takes its name from its whiteness (lucotis) due to the use of plaster. Some others think the name derives from lutek, a Celtic word referring to the marshes that line the banks of the Seine. Paris owes its name to the occupants of the site at the start of the Roman period: the Parisii. The presence of the river appears once again in "Par" which means boat; it remains the symbol borne on the City's coat of arms. Recent research shows that, before the arrival of the Romans, the cradle of local populations was not Lutetia but was instead near Nanterre.

In the Capital, almost all of the buildings are built of stone which distinguishes it from London, for example, where, apart from monuments, most of the housing is made of brick. The reason for this is geological. Limestone exists at a shallow depth below Paris, whereas in London there is "London clay", which is used to make bricks and tiles. The presence of limestone at a shallow depth under large Parisian areas also has an impact on infrastructure: this is why the metro tunnels could be "set down" at a very shallow depth, generally less than 7-8m.

The Capital takes up the centre of the Paris Basin **figure 2**) made up of layers of geological strata. The oldest strata (from the Triassic period, 250 million years ago) are found at a maximum depth of 3000m; the most recent are approximately 20 million years old. As an example, beneath the Eiffel Tower, the Jurassic base (dark blue layer in **figure 2**) is found at a depth of around 1800m. The buttes of Montmartre and Belleville mark the northern flank of an anticline. In Meudon, the anticline is plunging towards the Saint-Denis basin: chalk from the Cretaceous age is found at an altitude of +45m in Meudon, and at –80m in Saint-Denis.

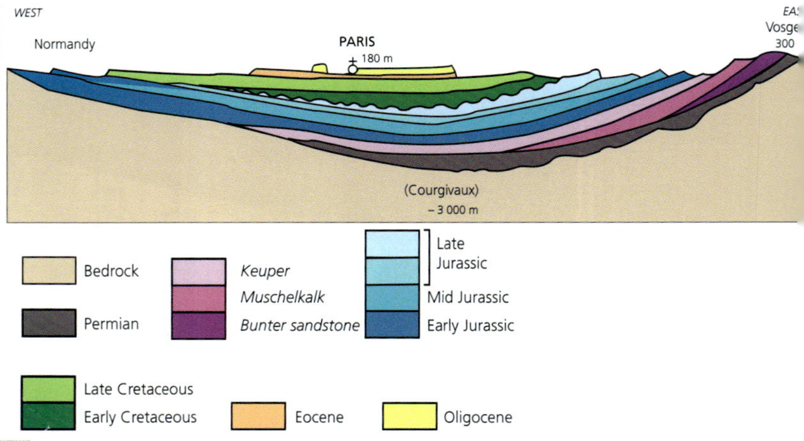

Fig. 2. W-E cross-section of Paris basin (according to Cavelier et al. 1980).

The city is located on terrain of the Tertiary - era where environments of particularly variable deposits gave rise to many kinds of rocks: limestone, clay, sand, gypsum and gritstone. In the centre of the Ile de France region, the city has developed by taking advantage of an exceptional geological site. From the level of the Seine at 26m, up to 128m at Rue du Télégraphe – an optical telegraph was installed there in 1792 – the river's cutting action has released almost all of the layers of tertiary rocks from the Parisian basin, thereby providing an abundance of usable rocks for building up the city. In addition, the Seine and its tributaries have deposited alluvium that is also useful (sand, clay, gravel).

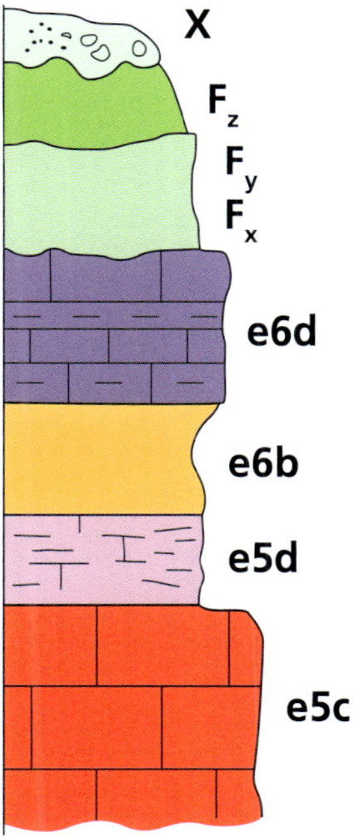

Fig. 3. Simplified geological diagram of the 5th arrondissement

X, $F_{x,y,z}$ group (**figure 3**) together the artificial embankments (**X**) that may exceed 5m in thickness and alluvium deposited by the watercourse ($F_{x,y,z}$). Recent alluvium (F_z) that is 5-8m thick correspond to silt found in the existing valley. The lower terrace (F_y) rises up to 10-15m above the current level of the watercourse, the mid-terrace (F_x) to 25-30m. They are made up of sand and gravel where siliceous elements (sandstone, flint, gritstone) are predominant. In the 5th arrondissement the most recent geological layer dating back to the early Bartonian (around 35 million years ago) is the limestone of Saint-Ouen, graded **e6d** and made up of lacustrine marls and limestone beds with a thickness of 10-15m. It forms a hard-wearing platform of which the fragments constitute the summit of Montagne Sainte-Geneviève. Below (**e6b**), the Beauchamp sands: they are multi-coloured and sometimes form sandstone. The "arènes de Lutèce" (Lutetian arenas) were dug into these sands. This is then followed by the Lutetian Age (40.4 to 48.6 million years ago) with two main levels. On top there are marls and scree (**e5d**) (approximately 10m). Below, there is coarse limestone (**e5c**) and its high quality beds, which we call the Parisian stone. If one were to observe the terrains that would span a trench excavated from the Seine to the Panthéon, this would show the overlay of the geological strata forming the sub-soil of the 5th arrondissement (**figure 4**).

The old course of the river Bièvre, the main Parisian tributary of the Seine, has been marked on the geological map (**figure 4**). Before arriving in the 5th arrondissement, the river crosses the 13th and its mouth, which is also located in this arrondissement, a little upstream from Pont d'Austerlitz. Between the courses of the Bièvre and the Seine, a blue dashed line on the geological map marks the location of a canal opened by the monks of the Abbey of Saint-Victor in 1148 to irrigate their gardens, established on the current site of the Jussieu Campus. This canal was possibly also used for transporting stones for the construction of Notre Dame. The canal opened into the Seine opposite Notre Dame at the site of Rue de Bièvre. It crossed the Philippe Auguste city wall through an archway revealed during the refurbishment of the post office on Rue du Cardinal Lemoine. It can be visited one day a week on Wednesdays. In 1361 a second canal was dug out that joined the Seine at Pont Sully.

Fig. 4. Simplified geological cross-section of rocks located beneath the 5th arrondissement.

Limestone quarries

The first quarries were opened by the Romans where the limestone was exposed, probably to supply the construction of the "thermes de Cluny" (thermal baths) and of the "arènes de Lutèce". These outcrops ran the length of the Bièvre's left bank. Other outcrops were quarried later at the bottom of the hill of Chaillot, on the right bank of the Seine. The progression of open-pit mining by eating away at hillsides also cut into the outer layers of limestone beds. This unusable overburden had to be removed. Consequently, in the 11th and 12th centuries, the quarry workers preferred to follow the limestone beds and dig into the hills. The quarries became underground. They could be reached from the ground level through entry points.

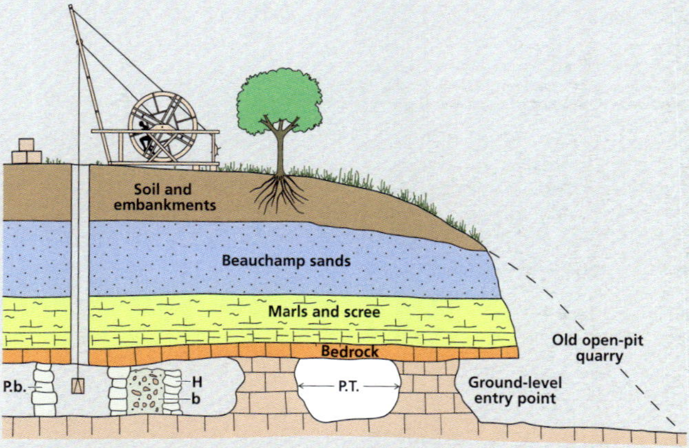

Fig. 5. Diagram of underground quarries in Paris.

There are two mining methods: with piliers tournés, or room and pillar, (P.T. in **figure 5**), the miners leave pillars of rock in place to support the roof of the mine. The open areas of the mine can be 7-8m high. This mining method was used by Parisian miners up until the 14th century. They then adopted the hagues et bourrages method: the roof of the mine was supported by dry stone pillars called "piliers à bras" (P.b. in **figure 5**), by stacking up blocks and by hagues et bourrages (H b in **figure 5**) which are dry-stone walls behind which waste from stone-cutting is piled up.

1) The starting point will be Place Jussieu*

Triangular in shape, Place Jussieu is lined with a single row of buildings with the two other sides being formed of the roads of Rue Linné and Jussieu. Among the buildings bordering Place Jussieu, numbers 5 and 7 (1842) are highly ornate: on one of them you will be able to recognise the bust of Henry II of France.

A few steps made of Burgundy limestone – Comblanchien stone from the Jurassic period – provide access to the esplanade of the university area. Well-polished, this hard rock becomes slippery when wet; this is why the edge of the steps is covered with an anti-slip strip. At the entrance you can access the University's mineral gallery, which is worth a visit for the beauty and diversity of the items displayed (1 to 2 hrs). Continue towards the right, following the balustrade along Rue Jussieu. Between towers 46 and 56, beyond a concrete flagstone, the paving is made of Lunel marble (from the Boulonnais, Carboniferous period) then black tiles break the uniformity and partially outline a church, the choir of which can be easily identified. It is the outline of the former church of Abbey Saint-Victor that was close to this spot in the 12th century. Around the choir, sarcophagus sites are represented by long black tiles.
The main entrance to the campus coincides with the main entrance to the abbey. The buildings were surrounded by a huge garden.

Travertine is a continental, vescular sedimentary limestone rock that is roughly stratified, with greater or lesser levels of concretion and usually yellowish to grey. The origin of travertine used in building is generally lacustrine. They can be lightly polished. The word travertine comes from Italian (travertine from Tivoli, from the Miocene epoch, is famous).

* See map inside back cover.

2) Jardin des Plantes

The royal garden for medicinal plants was founded in 1626 on land donated by Guy de la Brosse, Louis XIII's doctor. When it was opened in 1650, it was located in front of the buildings situated on the future Rue Geoffroy Saint-Hilaire. The lower half of the current garden was occupied by driftwood yards. It was smartened up by Fagon, Tournefort and Antoine de Jussieu, and became the Jardin du Roi in the 18th century. It was then significantly extended under the direction of Buffon who placed the natural history cabinet under the direction of Daubenton and the garden under that of André Thouin. It was the Convention that was responsible for the creation of the Muséum National d'Histoire Naturelle and the naming of the Jardin des Plantes.
Access the gardens through the official entrance at 57 Rue Cuvier.

Fig. 6. Sandstone paving blocks from Fontainebleau in the courtyard separating the garden entrance from the administration building.

The large size of the paving blocks (**figure 6**) bears witness to their great age. They are also not identical: some are convex, others are concave. The latter remained damp after a rainy period because the siliceous cement that binds their quartz grains does not fill in all the interstices. The rock therefore retains porosity that holds water. The cementation being incomplete, the rock is more fragile and erodes more easily.

At a height of 35m the butte Coypeau (**figure 7**) dominates the administration building. This is not a natural hill. It is a pile up of waste that accumulated there between 1190 and 1210 outside of the Philippe Auguste city wall that we will soon encounter (the wall not the king!). At the time, there was no organisation for handling waste!

Fig. 7. There is a belvedere at the summit of the butte Coypeau, and halfway up, you can find a bust of Théodore Monod. At the bottom of the butte an old basin can be seen, the base of which, among other things, bears beautiful ammonites.

Beneath the butte, the alpine garden (**figure 8**) opens out into an excavation, which extends towards the North through the bear pit. This provides a picture of an ancient open-pit stone quarry at the site of the current garden.

The progression of mining towards Montagne Sainte-Geneviève forced the quarry workers to clear infertile overburden that was increasingly thicker. Subsequently they decided to continue underground mining.

Fig. 8. The alpine garden, an ancient open-pit limestone quarry.

Short history of parisian paving blocks

In the Middle Ages, the unsurfaced streets of Paris turned into a muddy quagmire every time it rained. Most likely to eliminate the pungent odours rising from the streets close to his Louvre Palace, in 1186, Philippe Auguste decided to have the neighbouring streets covered with sandstone slabs 50 x 50cm in size with a thickness of 16 to 30cm. These slabs, which the workers cursed because they were heavy to handle, were gradually replaced in the 15th century with cubic sett paving blocks and then with King setts (pavés du roi), in 1730, measuring 8-9 inches i.e. 21 to 24cm sides. Their size decreased in the 19th century to 20cm sides: those are known as bâtards (lime-cement blocks). Their size continued to decrease until the 20th century (lack of strength among the Parisian pavers?): 10 x 10 x 16-19cm laid in a header course, vertically on a small face. The approximate age of a sett can therefore be judged from its size. The development of tyres has led Parisian pavers to abandon sandstone and replace it with granite. Nowadays, you often see recovered "sett edges" with 16-19cm sides but only 7-9cm thick.

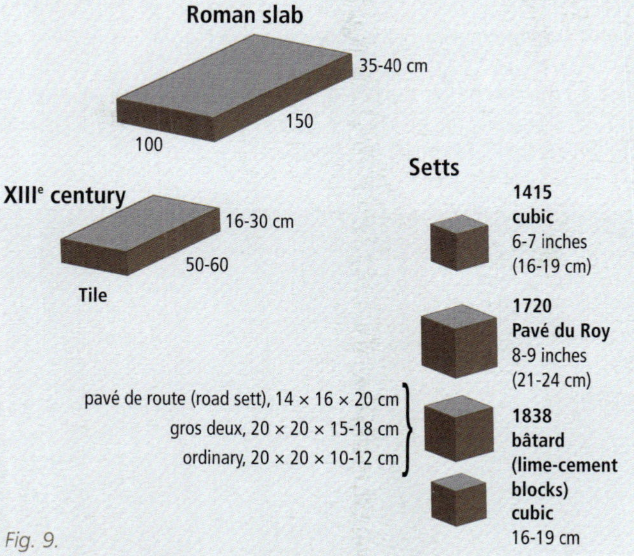

Fig. 9.

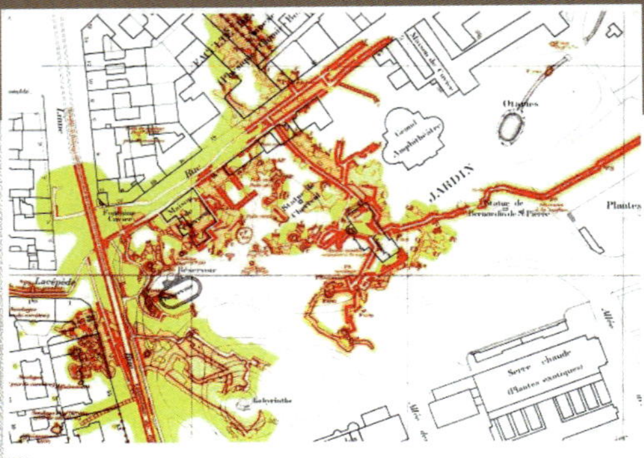

Fig. 10. Map of the Jardin des Plantes underground mines. The limestone still in place is in yellow, the built reinforcements are in red and the embankments are in dark brown.
Document: Inspection Générale des Carrières (General Quarry Inspection)

The entrance to this mine was a ground-level entrance (**figure 10**), located at the site of the zoological museum, opposite the library. Excavation work for the zoological museum was disrupted by boulders from the collapse of this entrance. The mining tunnels extended beyond the current Rue Linné that they now come up against. They were strengthened as of the 17th century. An access stairway was built behind the administration building. There was another access point on Rue Cuvier which is still visible. It is a shaft closed with a plate similar to manhole covers, with the letters I.D.C. (Inspection des carrières – Quarry inspection). The shaft is sealed off with a concrete plug to prevent trespassing. These mines were converted in 1900 by Armand VIRE, a speleologist, to set up the first underground zoology laboratory where cave-dwelling animals were studied.

Climb to the top of the butte Coypeau that has been converted into a maze. The path encircling the belvedere at the summit is edged with large blocks of gritstone (**figure 11**).

Fig. 11. Gritstone blocks close to the belvedere of the butte Coypeau.

Grifstone

Gritstone is a rock with extraordinary properties. It is almost pure silica, which makes it so hard. There are two types of gritstones. One, called cavernous, has lots of gaps but they do not come into contact with each other. Consequently the stone is not frost prone and makes very good thermal and sound insulation.

It was widely used for road metalling, in Parisian sewers and as a building stone: pavilions and non-residential buildings – schools, RATP (Paris Transport Authority) garages, EDF distribution centres, SNCF structures. The other type of gritstone, known as compact, was used for making grindstones, particularly around La Ferté-sous-Jouarre (Seine-et-Marne).

Fig. 12. Wall made from cavernous gritstone.

Fig. 13. Monolithic grindstone (approximately 1.8m diameter).

This rock with lots of crevices was widely used in the 19th century for creating rock gardens. Near the path, you can find the he tomb of Daubenton (1716-1800).

Gritstone was also used for constructing the wall underpinning the greenhouse on the right (**figure 14**) when you come down from the butte towards the *grande galerie*.

Fig. 14. The support wall of the greenhouses is made of gritstone interspersed with pilasters made from limestone of the Lutetian age.

Fig. 15. View of the facade of the Grande Galerie of the Muséum National d'Histoire Naturelle.

The Grande Galerie (figures 15-16)
It was built in the 19th century with large stonework ("grand appareil") made of Lutetian limestone, set on foundations made of limestone from Château-Landon, a more hard-wearing stone, known as "pierre froide" (cold stone) in French. The steps leading to the doorways are also made of Château-Landon limestone, in which we can see lots of round or elongated holes corresponding to imprints left by plants rooted at the bottom of the lake where the future limestone was deposited. It is easy to check the "coldness" of the Château-Landon limestone at the top of the steps where both types of rock can be seen. By placing one of your hands on one of the lower stones with the other hand on one of the stones higher up and leaving them there for a while, you will be able to notice that one of your hands cools down quicker than the other. The cooler of the two is the one that was placed on the cold stone. The "pierre froide" is less porous than the other and transfers heat quicker, while air contained in the porosity of the other stone acts as a thermal insulator.

*Fig. 16. Up closer, in the walls of the Grande Galerie, we can make out Château-Landon limestone at the bottom (**1**) and yellow limestone from the Lutetian age forming the height in large stonework ("grand appareil*") (**2**).*

*Appareil: (stonework) Arrangement of cut stones according to their dimension: sides measuring in the tens of centimetres = small stonework ("petit appareil"); sides measuring over 50–60cm = large stonework ("grand appareil")

Fig. 17. Château-Landon or Souppes-sur-Loing limestone.

Limestone from Château-Landon is a lacustrine limestone dating back to the Bartonian (Figure 1) that is light beige in colour. It is of very high quality, fine-grained and hard-wearing. It has a few round or elongated holes that correspond to ancient roots dispersed in the fine and homogeneous sediment before the rock hardened.

3) From the Jardin des Plantes to the Arènes de Lutèce

Go back up Rue Geoffroy-Saint-Hilaire along the gritstone garden wall. At the junction of Rue Cuvier there is the fountain (1671 and 1840) dedicated to Georges Cuvier. Made completely from Lutetian age limestone, the animal representation breaks the rules of the naturalists (Cuvier was one of them) by depicting a crocodile turning its head sideways, a movement that this animal's anatomy does not permit!

Fig. 18. Fountain dedicated to Cuvier made from Lutetian age limestone.

Before reaching Rue des Arènes continue a few more metres down Rue Linné which will allow you to see, at number 25, the old entrance to the "Maison des Eaux" that managed the Saint-Victor reservoir. The reservoir was built on the site of the lower part of the arena garden. Water from the Canal de l'Ourcq was then supplied through a pipe that crossed the Seine at Pont Sully. This is probably what supplied Fontaine Cuvier (**figure 18**).

At no. 5 Rue des Arènes you will find the house of Jean Paulhan (publicist) that is neogothic in style. The base is made from gritstone and height is Savonnieres limestone or lutetian limestone from Oise.

Fig. 19. Entrance to the Arènes de Lutèce.

The Arènes de Lutèce, built around the year 200, had 15,000 seats (**figure 19** p.15). Destroyed in the year 300 by the barbarians, they served as a quarry for stones, all already cut, for the Parisians. This is why, you may have read that the arenas occupied the site of a quarry. They were in fact cut out of the sands of Beauchamp that covered up the Lutetian limestone. They were restored in 1917. Cut blocks of Lutetian limestone are still abundant there. Large gritstone blocks were deposited to the right of the highest entrance.
In the garden there is a marble statue of Gabriel de Mortillet (1821-1898) who was an archaeologist. The base (**figure 20**) is made from Euville limestone. The organic debris that make up this rock from the Oxfordian age are arranged in fine layers (**figure 21**) the obliquity of which indicates the presence and the direction of underwater currents.

Fig. 20. Base made from biodetritic Euville limestone showing to the right.
Fig. 21. Traces of current from the sedimentation background.

4) From the Arènes de Lutèce to the Panthéon

Rue des Arènes leads to Rue de Navarre where you will find beautiful 19th century buildings made from Jurassic period Savonnières stone from Lorraine or Lutetian age limestone from Oise. Turn left into Rue Monge and follow until you reach the square of the same name. The course of the street dates back to the work started by Haussmann and the majority of the buildings present construction characteristics of the period (**figure 22**): the base made from Jurassic period cold limestone from Euville or limestone from Burgundy also of the Jurassic period, the height made from Lutetian age limestone or Savonnières stone.

Fig. 22. Typically Haussmannian buildings on Rue Monge.

Haussmannian buildings

Fig. 23.

Haussmann, who was appointed Prefect of the Seine in 1853 by Napoléon III, was responsible for town planning for 17 years. Wide roads were created, others were expanded. These operations led to the destruction of numerous houses that were replaced with constructions that benefited from new methods and made the best use of the stones' characteristics. The foundations and the belt course that sometimes sits on top of them are made from hard-wearing rocks with low porosity such as limestone from Euville, Burgundy or Château-Landon. The height of the facade walls are often Lutetian limestone from Oise or Savonnières stone (more porous and less hard-wearing). The foundation stones are at least twice as hard-wearing as the stones used for the height of the building. The foundation stones are less porous and therefore less heat-insulating. All it takes to be convinced of this is to place your hand on a higher up stone (provided that there is no paint) then on one of the foundation stones. The latter will seem colder, this is why in French it is known as "pierre froide" (cold stone). Furthermore, being less porous it avoids the rising of dampness by capillary action. The buildings have a metal structure. Another characteristic is the balconies on the 2nd and 5th (or 6th) floors, the last one often having a sloping ceiling. The facade was decorated with sculptures, first with sharp angles, then, from the 1900s onwards, with scrolled and rounded angles. The double-pitched roof has a steep roof break covered in slate (brisis) and a low-pitch zinc ridge (faîtage). This type of building was not limited to the period of the Second French Empire, they carried on building like this until the wake of the First World War. The similar looking "Haussmannian" buildings gives a remarkable degree of unity to lots of roads in Paris.

Fig. 24.

At no. 14, there is a curious house decorated with sculpted tools suggesting the association between builders and stone masons.

The facade of the barracks in Place Monge is made from Savonnières stone on a Euville limestone foundation. The upper part is built from brick.

To the right of the barracks, Rue Ortolan runs along an older part of the barracks which is made from Lutetian age limestone. You can see ancient graffiti at the bottom of the wall (**figure 25**).

Can you read them, date them? They are all located close to the ground. They were probably carved at shoulder height when the street level was lower before being filled in and built up as was the case with many ancient streets.

Fig. 25. Graffiti on Rue Ortolan.

Rue Ortolan comes out on Rue Mouffetard that gets its name from "mouffettes" (skunks in French), or mofetta, putrid odours given off by refuse and wastewater that are now fortunately a thing of the past! The main materials in these ancient districts are Lutetian limestone and plaster. The back walls of the barracks (no. 61) have red speckles. These are not fossils but remains of plaster intended to plug holes in the stone. The fountain (1671) on the corner of Rue du Pot de Fer is also made of Parisian stone.

Go back up Rue Mouffetard until you reach Place de la Contrescarpe then take Rue du Cardinal Lemoine to Rue Clovis and follow it towards the Panthéon (**figure 26**).
On the way you will come across a part of the Philippe Auguste wall completed in 1213. It is approximately 3m thick at the base, 9m high, and has a core of rubble and mortar filling the space between the exterior and interior walls constructed in small Paris stonework.

Fig. 26. Rue Clovis: part of the Lutetian age limestone Philippe Auguste wall.

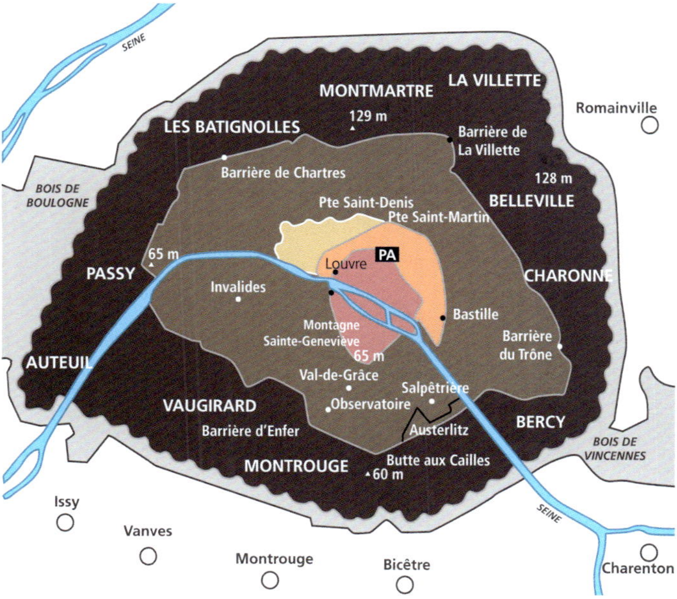

Fig. 27. Succession of Paris city walls.

The Philippe Auguste wall (**PA** on **figure 27**) was built in 1213 and extended in 1383 by Charles V and went on to cover the new Bastille fortress.

Fig. 28. Parisian pavements.

The bluish grey granite from Vire forms the main part of pavement curbs (**figure 28**). In former times, at road junctions, the dropped curb for making crossing easier for prams, scooters, etc. was made with granite that was pinker and had larger crystals. This granite was from Flamanville. This is the case at the crossroads of Rue Clovis and Rue Descartes.

All about granite

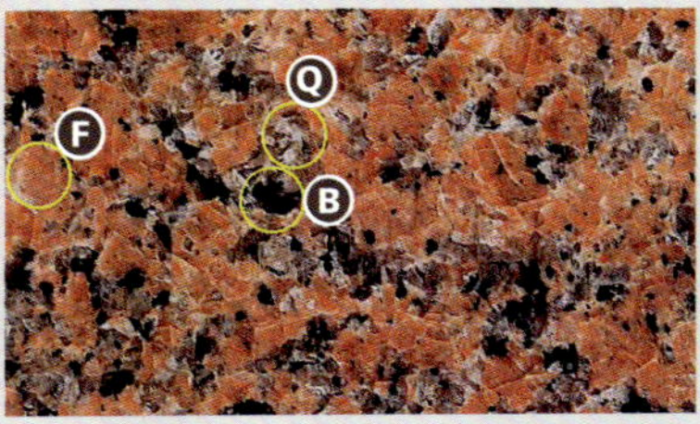

Fig. 29. Clarté Granite.

Granite is a rock that results from the cooling down of magma (pool of highly viscous molten rock) at depth (4-5km). It consists mainly of three minerals: feldspar (**F**), mica (**B**) and quartz (**Q**).
The sample pictured is a common ornamental stone in Paris. This is the rock known as Clarté pink granite from the name of a town located next to Perros-Guirec Ploumanach (Côte d'Armor).

Fig. 30. Savonnières Stone.

Savonnières stone (Meuse) is from the Tithonian age. It is a very fine-grained oolitic limestone containing a few shells. From beige to off-white in colour, we can see lots of little holes that appear black in the picture. This is a stone that was often used for putting up buildings in the 19th century.

The Paris of 1280 had 310 streets (like the current town of Rambouillet), covered 250 hectares and had approximately 220,000 inhabitants. Today there are around 5218 streets in Paris.
Rue Clovis is then bordered by the Saint-Etienne du Mont church (**figure 31**) and the Lycée Henri IV (**figure 32**) (secondary school): both are built from Paris stone.

Fig. 31. The Saint-Etienne du Mont church is mainly built of Lutetian age limestone ("the stone of Paris").

Fig. 32. Rue Clovis, Lycée Henri IV and the tower of the old Abbey of Sainte-Geneviève. The dome of the Panthéon can be seen in the background. Lots of Lutetian age limestone can be found in these buildings.

Rue Clovis comes out onto Place Sainte-Geneviève which is an extension of Place du Panthéon. To the right a few steps lead to the entrance of the Saint-Etienne du Mont church, the rood screen of which, unique in Paris, is worth a look. The dark colour of the steps contrasts with the lighter stones of the building (**figure 33**). There are made with Volvic stone, a volcanic rock called "andesite" that was used for constructing Clermont-Ferrand cathedral. We are now a long way from the stones of the Paris region!
The steps are more recent than the church because Place Sainte-Geneviève was renovated in 1805 and then in 1843-1844. In 1805, the Prefect was Comte Chabrol de Volvic.

Fig. 33. Façade of Saint-Etienne du Mont. The building is made from Lutetian limestone from Oise, the steps are made from Volvic stone (a lava).

5) The Panthéon

The Panthéon (1782), which used to be the Sainte-Geneviève church, stands majestically, at a height of 83m, on Montagne Sainte-Geneviève, which in Roman times was called *Mons Leucotitius* and was crowned by the temple of Mercury.

Volvic Stone

The age of this lava is less than 10,000 years. Its use in Paris dates from the time when Joseph Gaspard Chabrol de Volvic was the Prefect of Paris, at the start of the 19th century. This engineer accompanied Bonaparte to Egypt. Being highly involved and convinced of the quality of Volvic stone, he created a school of architecture in Volvic. This stone can be cut into large slabs and Chabrol de Volvic came up with the idea of enamelling the rock to make street nameplates with it. The first enamelling workshop was founded in Paris.

The Lutetian age limestone blocks for this huge work came, for the most part, from Conflans Sainte-Honorine in the Yvelines department. Beneath the northern face, opposite the Sainte-Geneviève library, on a flight of steps we can see a little used rock that is reddish brown, riddled with tubes (from worms?) with a lighter filling and showing lots of traces of fossils (**figures 34-35**).

Fig. 34-35. Limestone rich in traces of fossils at the Panthéon.

Fig. 36. Main entrance to the Panthéon, a catalogue of rocks.

The paving (**figure 36**) leading to the main entrance stairway of the monument again uses Volvic stone (**V**) coupled with Château-Landon limestone (**C**), the whiteness of which contrasts with the dark grey of the lava. The sett paving stones are Fontainebleau sandstone (**G**).
The steps are made from Lutetian bedrock (**figure 37** p.24).
The paving also includes marble from Soignies (small granite). Between the pillars, the paving stones are made from granite from Vire and Flamanville as well as Comblanchian type limestone from Burgundy.

Fig. 37. The main entrance steps of the Panthéon are made of bedrock, a high-quality Lutetian limestone. It contains lots of shells and traces from a small gastropod (ceriths).

6) From the Panthéon to the Val-de-Grâce

From Place du Panthéon take Rue d'Ulm to the south. From no. 2 to no. 6, there are beautiful buildings from the end of the 19th century in Lutetian stone from Oise. At the crossroads with Rue Lhomond, there is the Résidence Lhomond with its foundations coated with a green marble stone, serpentine breccia (see boxed text) originating from Italy. At no. 15 the Franco-Lebanese hall of residence is covered perpendicularly with travertine. A little bit further, the old buildings of the Ecole Normale Supérieur, at no. 45, are built with large Lutetian stonework from Oise. Rue d'Ulm comes out on Rue Claude Bernard, the appearance of which is very similar to that of Rue Monge. The road that was opened in the 19th century is lined with buildings of stone from Oise or Savonnières on foundations of "pierre froide" limestone (Euville). A little detour to no. 16 shows the Institut National Agronomique built in brick with Savonnières stone quoins. The foundations combine Euville limestone and gritstone rubbles. Head back up Rue Claude Bernard onto Rue des Feuillantines then Rue Saint-Jacques to the left until you reach Place Alphonse Laverand, situated opposite Val-de-Grâce, which is made of Lutetian age limestone.

Anne of Austria expressed a wish to have a magnificent church built as soon as she had a son. On 5 September 1638, the future Louis XIV was born. The wish was fulfilled, and in 1639 construction of the church was entrusted to François Mansart. Mansart was aware of the mine voids beneath the proposed location for the construction. In 1639, he drew up maps of the mines and reinforcement work began in 1645 (**figures 38-39**). This considerable amount of work took up most of the amount set aside. The walls of the nave are only 11 metres high. Mansart was removed from the construction work to be replaced by Lemercier and then Pierre le Muet. The Val-de-Grâce church was completed in 1667 (**figure 40**).

Fig. 38-39. Mansart's reinforcements under Val-de-Grâce.

Fig. 40. Val-de-Grâce.

The dome is an imitation of that of Saint-Peter's Basilica in Rome. There is lots of marble inside the church. The marble of the altar is black, veined with white and comes from Barbençon in the Avesnois. Visiting the church is unfortunately restricted.
The site has been a military hospital since 1850.

Serpentine, greenstone, green marble, peridotitee

Serpentine results from alterations in specific igneous rocks, peridotites. These rocks are the main components of the Earth's mantle (over 30-35km deep). As soon as they come close to the ocean floor, they are subjected to hot hydrothermal fluids. This is seawater that has gone down into the rocks through fractures and has heated up at depth. The peridotites are then more or less completely transformed into fibrous minerals. We end up with a dark green stone with lighter twisted veins that are reminiscent of snakeskin, hence the name serpentine. It is a soft stone that is quite easy to polish and is often used in facing. It is often called green marble with various qualifiers.

Fig. 41. Building covered with slabs of serpentine.

7) Église Saint-Jacques-du-Haut-Pas

Pick up Rue Saint-Jacques again and head towards the Seine. At no. 251, we can see facing made from Scandinavian red granite and green serpentine (Maurin green from Haute Ubaye).

Église Saint-Jacques-du-Haut-Pas was built in 1584, and extended in 1630. Its enlargement required the reversal of its orientation, making it one of the rare Parisian churches with the choir facing towards the West. The building made from Lutetian limestone from Oise includes some beautiful marble items.

Fig. 42. Altar of église Saint-Jacques-du-Haut-Pas.

The top of the altar (**figure 42**) is made of Jurassic Comblanchien limestone from Burgundy. The band is griotte (red and brown speckled marble) from Félines. The small columns are breccia – Brocatelle from Spain. The panels, which are also made from violet breccia, are surrounded by green Aver marble. The grey marble above the altar stone and surrounding the tabernacle is Bardiglio Fiorito marble. The tabernacle door is made from Spanish Brocatelle. Lastly, to the left of the altar beneath the statue of the Virgin Mary, there is a yellow brocatelle marble panel. In short, a large selection of marbles.

Marbles

For geologists this is an old limestone that has recrystallised as a result of an increase in temperature and pressure generally associated with tectonic movements (formation of mountain ranges). It is a metamorphic rock. For a marble setter, it is a fine-grained stone, typically limestone, that can be polished, whatever its origin.

Stucco

This is a natural render consisting of lime mixed with sand, marble or brick dust mixed with a plant or animal based binder. Egg white was widely used in the past.

Jacques-Denis Cochin, one of the priests of the church left his name to posterity by creating a hospice that became Hôpital Cochin and is nearby but located in the 14th arrondissement.
Continue along Rue Saint-Jacques. At the crossroads with Rue Gay-Lussac, we can see the dropped pavement with a block of Flamanville granite where the feldspars are clearly angled. After crossing Rue Soufflot, Rue Saint-Jacques descends (towards the Seine) and runs along past Lycée Louis le Grand, the foundation of which is made from Burgundy stone (oolitic limestone with stylolite) and Euville stone. The height of the building is made from Savonnières stone or Lutetian age limestone.

Oolitic limestone

Fig. 43. Oolitic limestone.

The name comes from its resemblance to fish eggs (Oon in Greek). Oolites: millimetric-sized spheres composed of concentric layers. In the centre, a grain of sand or fossil fragment can be found. Around the edge: the rings of limestone are the work of bacteria. This common type of rock indicates a disturbed and shallow depositional environment.

8) The Sorbonne and Cluny

Opposite the lycée is the Sorbonne (**figures 44-45**) that we skirt around on Rue Cujas then Rue Victor Cousin to arrive at Place de la Sorbonne. Opposite the "Select Hôtel" granite paving stones from Sidobre cover the ground. The Sorbonne church is the oldest part of the building (1635). If the door is open, you can go and see the columns of the choir made from Rance marble (a reef limestone from the Belgian Ardennes). The whole thing is made from Lutetian age limestone from Oise.

Fig. 44 and 45. The Sorbonne chapel made from Lutetian age limestone.

The modern part of the Sorbonne (1895-1901) (**figures 46-47**) judiciously uses more resistant limestone known as "cold stone" in French for the foundations. This feature is clearly visible on the facade of Rue des Ecoles.

*Fig. 46 and 47. The modern part of the Sorbonne from the Rue des Écoles side. The foundations (**1**) made from Château-Landon limestone are topped (**2**) with 4 rows of Euville limestone. We can see Lutetian age limestone in the remainder of the height (**3**) up to the roof covered with slate. At number 16 on Rue de la Sorbonne, Vilhonneur (Charente) limestone has been used.*

False bed

The bedding of a sedimentary rock corresponds to small changes in deposition. These discontinuities lead to a change in the rock's mechanical properties. The beds are more or less hard-wearing. When the stone is laid normally with the beds parallel to the ground, these differences in resistance are not dangerous. But if the rock is on false-bed, perpendicularly to the bedding, the different beds run the risk of disjoining. The rock splits. In constructions with cut stones the blocks are generally laid "normally". Some very hard-wearing rocks, such as Lutetian age liais, may be laid on false-bed. However, in most cases, a false-bed rock we might see is a facing, with a slice of rock a few centimetres thick stuck or hooked onto a wall.

Square Paul Painlevé separates the Sorbonne from Hôtel de Cluny dating back to 1490. This "hôtel" is built with Lutetian limestone from Saint-Leu (Oise) with small stonework. The courtyard (**figure 48**) is paved with sandstone from Fontainebleau and the roof is covered with slate.

Fig. 48. Inner courtyard of Hôtel de Cluny.

Adjoining the Hôtel de Cluny, the Roman baths (2nd and 3rd centuries) (**figure 49**) are the oldest building in Paris. Made from Parisian limestone, very hard liais and cliquart that originated most likely from the banks of the Bièvre, it is also decorated with courses of red bricks. Recent reinforcements that are visible from Boulevard Saint-Michel also used Lutetian limestone from Saint-Maximin but with large stonework.

Fig. 49. The "thermes de Cluny" seen from Boulevard Saint-Michel.

Bricks and tiles

The production of bricks and tiles can be divided into five stages: extraction of clay, preparation of clay mix, shaping or moulding, drying and firing. The clay is mixed with water and the soft mix is drawn out and left in a special storage area (pourrissoir). The finely ground clay is then fed into the funnel of the moulding machine. The shape imposed on the clay varies depending on the desired product. The kiln is the heart of the brickyard. The batch is subject to heating that increases regularly up to the firing temperature (between 850 and 1200°C depending on the clay used), and then must cool down equally gradually. For tiles, the temperature is always higher than 1000°C and the minimum firing duration is 20 hours.
In Paris and the surrounding area, various geological clay formations such as "plastic" ball clay from the Ypresian age were used for making tiles and bricks. There were lots of quarries in the Vaugirard district. Pockets of clay that you can find in the alluvium of the Seine were also used, particularly in the Tuileries district.

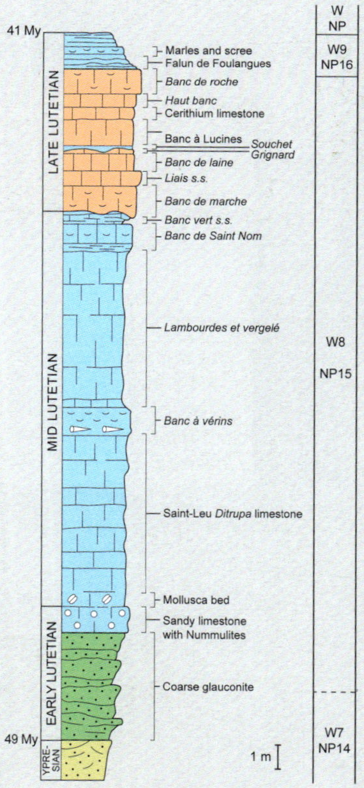

Fig. 50. Overview cross section of the Lutetian age (according to J.P.Gély 1998).

Lutetian age

Part of the ground located beneath Paris brought about a division in the geological time scale, called the Lutetian age, after the Roman name for the Capital (Lutetia). Several levels were mined starting from Roman times, first with quarries then with underground mines as evidenced by the Thermes de Cluny and the Arènes de Lutèce in the 5th arrondissement
In the higher levels, the most beautiful stones originated from the "Bancs francs" (even-grained siliceous limestone) the thin layers of which provided small stonework (in the tens of centimetres). The "Bed-rock" was never mined because it formed the roof of the mines. Common on the embankments, it came from open-pit quarries. A hard and resistant stone was extracted from the base of the upper level: "Liais". Its thickness, in the decimetre range, made it a good choice of material for making the oldest Parisian tombstones. Its fineness and resistance are such that it was used in false bed. The mid-level provided larger size stones (in the metre range) extracted from the "Lambourdes et Vergelé". Operations at this level under Paris were not very extensive due to the presence of the water table that limited the mining of it.

9) Ronsard and the Pleïade

Place Marcellin Berthelot opposite the Collège de France (made from Lutetian limestone) is embellished with a bust of Ronsard to the glory of the Pleïade group of poets (**figure 51**). The pedestal of the bust is very interesting. The crinoidal limestone (Euville limestone) is very weathered on the western side that is most exposed to bad weather. The names of the poets have almost faded away from it. Weathering has not only had negative effects, as it has revealed the component elements of the limestone: spines of sea urchins, isolated crinoid fossils in the form of a five-pointed star (**figure 52**) recalling the 5-point radial-symmetry of Echinodermata.

*Fig. 51. The bust of Ronsard made from Euville limestone consisting in particular of beautiful crinoid fossils (**figure 52**).*

Fig. 52. Crinoid fossils visible in the Euville limestone.

Along Rue des Ecoles, which is lined with Haussmannian buildings, at no. 2bis you can see an exceptional building that was entirely built from gritstone in 1895. On the opposite side, at no. 3, there is a building from 1869 that has a beautiful finely crafted facade. There is another building (1905) made completely from gritstone at no. 5 Rue des Lyonnais.

Opposite the Collège de France take Rue Jean de Beauvais as far as Boulevard Saint-Germain, where you will again find the Haussmannian style embellished with the classic eclecticism of the end of the 19th century: caryatids (no. 21 and 80) ionic or Corinthian columns and pilasters (no. 21 and 64).
From Place Maubert take Rue Lagrange then Rue Galande. This is the Paris of days gone by. Here we can see well-established houses (no. 31 and 33). The route takes us close to Rue Domat, formerly Rue des Plâtriers due to the houses covered with plaster produced by heating gypsum from Montmartre.
We then arrive at Rue Saint-Julien le Pauvre and its church (**figure 53**). The first building that was destroyed by the Normans in 806 was rebuilt with Lutetian age cliquart from the banks of the Bièvre. Nearby, in Square René Viviani there is a black locust tree that was planted by Jean Robin in 1602, undoubtedly the oldest tree in Paris. Here you can also see an old well.

Fig. 53. Eglise Saint-Julien-le-Pauvre, one of the oldest in Paris made from Lutetian age limestone.

These formerly numerous wells were sources of water for Parisians but the overflow of waste water and ditches (that were far from being sewage pipes), made their water neither good nor safe to drink. It was replaced in the 16th century by water from the fountains supplied by aqueducts.

Cross Rue Saint-Jacques to reach Eglise Saint-Séverin. This beautiful church, with a magnificent choir, is made from Lutetian limestone from the mines of Faubourg Saint-Jacques and Montsouris then of Saint-Leu and Trossy. Stone from Trossy, close to Saint-Maximin in Oise, was used from the 12th century. In front of the church on Rue des Prêtres Saint-Séverin, which opens up at the site of the old Saint-Séverin cemetery, it is possible to make reference to another type of "stone". In 1461, this was where the first operation for kidney stones took place on someone sentenced to death, who then survived and was pardoned by Louis XI.

10) The banks of the Seine from Rue Saint-Jacques to Pont de la Tournelle

Pick up Rue Saint-Jacques again, turn right along Quai de Montebello and follow it until Rue de Bièvre. This road takes its name not from the river, but from the canal that joined the Seine at this point. In the old days, the canal crossed the Philippe Auguste wall through an archway revealed during the reconstruction of the post office at the corner of Rue des Ecoles and Rue des Fossés Saint-Bernard. At the corner of this road, we can see one of the oldest levelling plaques in Paris, dating back to the 19th century (**figure 54**). The levelling of Paris is calculated based on the water level of the Bassin de la Villette: 51.49m to which we add 50m (101.49m) and subtract the elevation above sea level. Why make it simple.... The lowest water level of the course of the Seine corresponds to the zero of the Pont de la Tournelle built during the low-water period of 1719.

Fig. 54. Old levelling plaque of Paris at the corner of Rue des Ecoles and Rue des Fossés Saint-Bernard.

A little further along, Pont de l'Archevêché (**figure 55**) provides a spectacular view over the apse of Notre Dame. The parapet that bears the nameplate deserves attention. It is made of limestone from the Bedrock, a hard bed that typically forms a strong roof for the mines, as the higher levels were unsound. There are therefore grounds to think that these stones came from an open-pit quarry outside of Paris. The walls of the "Ile de la Cité" that are facing us are made of gritstone with Lutetian limestone pilasters.

Fig. 55. Pont de l'Archevêché and Notre Dame de Paris.

Continue along Quai de la Tournelle. At no. 47 there is the Musée de l'Assistance Publique (**figure 56**), the former convent of the Miriamones, nuns who looked after poor young girls. Its construction is classical: slate roof, building made from Lutetian age yellow limestone, courtyard paved with sandstone from Fontainebleau.

Fig. 56. The Musée de l'Assistance Publique at no. 57 Quai de la Tournelle.

11) Pont de la Tournelle, Collège des Bernardins

Continuing along Quai de la Tournelle (**figure 57**), we will arrive at the bridge with the same name, dominated by the statue of Sainte-Geneviève, the patron saint of Paris. This marks the end of our journey. The bridge has remained very white despite the pollution, as it was built with the same stone as the Sacré-Cœur Basilica of Montmartre: Château-Landon limestone. The Tournelle was a square fort built in 1359. The Philippe Auguste wall continued up to the current Pont Sully opposite which the gate of Saint-Bernard opened.

Fig. 57. Pont de la Tournelle built from Château-Landon limestone that whitens with age!

We are very close to Collège des Bernardins on Rue de Poissy. Don't miss the chance to go and admire the grand refectory that has been magnificently restored and open to the public since September 2008. The whole of the building is made from Lutetian limestone.

The building that was built in the 12th and 14th centuries for the Cistercian (or Bernardine) (**figure 58**) monks was seized during the Revolution in 1790 in order to become national property. After being used as a fire station then as a dormitory for the Police school, it was bought by the Paris diocese in 2001 who had it renovated between 2004 and 2008 to make it a Catholic debate centre.

Fig. 58. Collège des Bernardins, magnificently restored.

From there, it is easy to get back to the starting point by Rue de Poissy, Rue des Ecoles and Rue Jussieu.

Translation by RAPTRAD - RSO (Toulouse). Thanks to Éric Lorigny (CNES) for his intercession.

Map of the Geolo
arrondisse

biotope ÉDITIONS

LES ÉDITIONS DU MUSÉUM

SGF Société Géologique de France
Des géologues au service de la société

IUGS GTG Geoheritage Task Group

UNESCO Organisation des Nations Unies pour l'éducation, la science et la culture · avec le soutien de la Commission nationale française pour l'UNESCO

To order:
Biotope
22, boulevard Maréchal Foch
34140 Mèze
Tel.: 04 67 18 65 39
Fax: 04 67 18 46 29
www.leclub-biotope.com

Dépôt légal décembre 2015

Conception et réalisation :
BIOTOPE
Secrétariat d'édition : **Grégoire Egoroff (MNHN, geopatrimoine@mnhn.fr)**
Impression :
Pure Impression (France)

Bibliographic reference to be used:

OBERT D., STEINBERG M., DARTIGUES J.-C., 2012 – *Geological Walk in the 5th* arrondissement of Paris. Biotope, Mèze - MNHN, Paris (Collection Balades géologiques), 42 pages.

Pictures are owed to the authors with the exception of pictures 2, 3, 4, 5 and 50 (drawing by Alexandre Lethiers, UPMC).

Cover: Val-de-Grâce.
Above: Saint-Etienne du Mont, the only Parisian church with a rood screen.

Prix TTC : 4 €

9 782366 621693

ISBN BIOTOPE: 978-2-36662-169-3
ISSN: 2109-9332

PEFC 10-31-1244 Certifié PEFC pefc-france.org